Perfection of Character

PERFECTION OF CHARACTER
GUIDING PRINCIPLES FOR
THE MARTIAL ARTS & EVERYDAY LIFE

TERUYUKI OKAZAKI

GMW PUBLISHING

Philadelphia, Pennsylvania

Perfection of Character. Copyright ©2006 by Teruyuki Okazaki. All rights reserved. No part of this book may be used, reproduced, or transmitted in any form, or by any means, electronic or mechanical, including photocopying, recording, or by way of any other information storage and/or retrieval system, in any manner whatsoever without written permission from the publisher, except for the inclusion of brief quotations in critical articles and reviews. For information, please address GMW Publishing, P.O. Box 34585, Philadelphia, PA 19101-4585

Perfection of Character is available at special quantity discounts for business, sales promotion, and educational use. For information, please write to: Sales Department, GMW Publishing, P.O. Box 34585, Philadelphia, PA 19101-4585

The material contained within this book is informational only.

Published and distributed in the United States by GMW Publishing
Designed by Hiroyoshi Okazaki
Produced in collaboration with Eric Ackland
Printed on acid free paper
Printed in Canada

First Edition / First Print: November 2006
 10 9 8 7 6 5 4 3 2 1

Library of Congress Control Number: 2006932021

ISBN-13: 978-0-9785763-2-5
ISBN-10: 0-9785763-2-2

Dedicated to my teachers Master Gichin Funakoshi and Master Masatoshi Nakayama

Acknowledgements

I would like to thank Mr. Hiroyoshi Okazaki, Mr. Robert Sandler, Ms. Lois Luzi, Mr. Christopher Carew, and Mr. Gregory Weinberg for helping me with this book.

Contents

Introduction 1

Dojo Kun 3

Seek perfection of character 7
Jinkaku kansei ni tsutomuro koto

Be faithful 13
Makoto no michi o mamoru koto

Endeavor 17
Doryoku no seishin o yashinau koto

Respect others 21
Reigi o omonzuru koto

Refrain from violent behavior 27
Kekki no yu o imashimuru koto

Niju Kun 31

1- **Do not forget that karate begins
   with a bow and finishes with a bow** 35
   Karate-do wa rei ni hajimari rei ni owaru koto o wasureruna

2- **In karate, never attack first** 43
   Karate ni sente nashi

3- **One who practices karate must follow the way of justice** .. 49
   Karate wa gi no tasuke

4- **Know yourself first, then you can know others** 55
   Mazu jiko o shire, shikoshite ta o shire

5- **Spirit and mind are more important than technique** 63
   Gijutsu yori shinjutsu

6- **Be ready to release your mind** 69
   Kokoro wa hanatan koto o yosu

7- **Misfortune comes out of idleness** 77
   Waza wai wa ketai ni seizu

8- **Don't think that what you learn in karate
   can't be used outside the dojo** 83
   Dojo nomino karate to omouna

9- It will take all of your life to learn karate 89
   Karate no shugyo wa issho

10- Put karate into your everyday living;
    that is how to see its true beauty 95
    Ara yuru mono o karateka seyo; soko ni myomi ari

11- Karate is just like hot water;
    if you do not give it continuous heat, it will become cold 101
    Karate wa yu no gotoshi taezu netsu o ataezareba moto no mizu ni kaeru

12- Do not cling to the idea of winning;
    it is the idea of not losing that is necessary 107
    Katsu kangae wa motsuna; makenu kangae wa hitsuyo

13- Move according to your opponent 113
    Teki ni yotte tenka seyo

14- In conflict, you must discern the vulnerable
    from the invulnerable points 117
    Tatakai wa kyo-jitsu no soju ikan ni ari

15- Consider your opponent's legs and arms as
    you would lethal swords 123
    Hito no te-ashi o ken to omoe

16- Be aware at all times that you have
    millions of potential opponents 129
    Danshi mon o izureba hyakuman no teki ari

17- Postured stance is for beginners; later comes naturalness 133
    Kamae wa shoshinsha ni atowa shizen-tai

18- Kata is about correct and proper form;
    engaging in a real fight is something else 139
    Kata wa tadashiku, jisen wa betsumono

19- Do not forget: 1) strength and weakness of power; 2) contraction
    and expansion of body; and 3) rhythm of techniques 145
    Chikara no kyojaku, tai no shinshuku, waza no kankyu o wasureruna

20- Always create and devise 151
    Tsune ni shinen kufu seyo

Conclusion 157

Glossary 159

About the Author 163

Introduction

Karate practitioners and other martial artists must know that the martial arts are about more than physical development, self-defense, and competition; most importantly, they are about continually striving to perfect one's character. My teacher, Master Gichin Funakoshi, lived by and taught this philosophy, and his example has inspired me to write this book.

Master Funakoshi gave us the *Dojo Kun* and the *Niju Kun* as guides to pursuing the perfection of character. The *Dojo Kun* are the five guiding, general principles of karate; and the *Niju Kun* are the 20 more detailed, subordinate principles of karate, which encompass morality, technique, and proper mindset. In karate schools throughout the world, students recite the *Dojo Kun* after class, but the *Niju Kun* is often left unlearned. It is my sincere wish to bring understanding of the *Niju Kun*, as well as the *Dojo Kun*, back into the daily mindset of karate students and martial artists throughout the world.

As you read this book, you will come to understand the value and meaning of these precepts, and how they can be incorporated into your everyday life. If every martial artist will meditate deeply on these principles regularly, he or she will grow morally, spiritually, and technically, and will become a more effective agent in the quest to mend the world.

Dojo Kun

Calligraphy by Master Masatoshi Nakayama

The *Dojo Kun* are the five guiding principles of karate. In class, before we repeat each precept of the *Dojo Kun*, we say the word *hitotsu*. The Japanese character for *hitotsu* is a single horizontal line, which means one. Why do we say "one" before each principle instead of progressively counting to five? Master Funakoshi may have wished to emphasize that they are all of equal importance, and that though they are stated separately and progressively, they are all to be considered as one comprehensive whole.

Saying *hitotsu* is also a way to focus the mind and recite the precept with more conviction and spirit. Furthermore, when we recite these five *Dojo Kun* precepts aloud in class, we do it in unison, which reinforces the idea that the karate community is united as one. Perhaps this is also part of what Master Funakoshi meant.

As you read *Perfection of Character*, please keep in mind that I am sharing my interpretations of Master Funakoshi's principles. In the course of studying and practicing them, I am certain that you will also develop your own unique understanding of their meaning and value.

Seek perfection of character
Jinkaku kansei ni tsutomuro koto

No one is perfect, and perfection is impossible, so what can it possibly mean to seek perfection of character? What can it mean to seek perfection in anything? It simply means that in every moment, we must be striving to become better human beings. Seeking perfection of character means knowing that there is always room to grow and improve, and purposefully acting to do so.

Every day, karate students worldwide say the *Dojo Kun* after training. We do this so that we can keep these goals in mind, and accelerate our spiritual transformation. Initially you might study karate solely for physical motivations, but gradually you should gain insight as to why you are practicing those things, and your motives will subtly change. For most of us, physical motivations will dominate, but if we can become just 10 percent motivated by the goal of spiritual growth and self-improvement, we will have already achieved something extraordinary.

Sometimes (perhaps always) you don't think deeply about the *Dojo Kun* when you say it; nevertheless it penetrates into your subconscious mind. Just as we must practice and repeat *kata* (prearranged forms using karate techniques against multiple, imaginary opponents) hundreds, and even thousands of times before they become second nature, so too must we repeat our guiding philosophy as many times, so that it also becomes second nature to us. You must always say the *Dojo Kun* with as much conscious intention, conviction, and focus as possible. Always repeat these words as if it were the first time, and as if you are making a solemn oath, for that is in fact what you are doing.

When we test for higher ranking in karate, one of the most important things that we look at is character development. Has the individual become a better person? We look at a person's attitude towards bowing, whether he or she helps others, whether he or she is respectful and humble. Improvement in technique is important of course, however, if that is all that has changed, I cannot pass a person to a higher level. His or her character must change as well.

Sometimes a younger person may not have the maturity to be passed to a higher level despite having excellent technique. He or she will need greater life experience to progress to a higher level. It can be frustrating not to be able to take a grading exam when you know you have the requisite skill, however, it is important to know that you are always being gauged for character development. I myself had to test three times to receive my *shodan* (first/beginning level black belt) before Master Funakoshi passed me. Trust me, your *sensei* (instructor) can see whether you are ready. Have patience and trust, and take the long-term view. Don't train to advance a belt; train to become the best level belt that you've already attained. Always seek to perfect your character.

Be faithful
Makoto no michi o mamoru koto

Most precisely translated, this principle means that there is a path of truth and sincerity that you must guard and defend. Faithfulness implies a commitment, and it is only through commitment that one can excel in anything. We need to make a commitment to practicing karate, and to being a truthful, responsible member of the karate community. Being faithful also implies being tactful, kind, and sincere.

Faithfulness means practicing daily, arriving on time, and showing respect to everyone even when doing these things is difficult, and you don't want to do them. In fact, unless we struggle, commitment and faithfulness have little meaning. A marriage, for example, isn't a marriage if at the first sign of difficulty one person abandons the other. Commitment truly means "for better or for worse, in sickness and in health, for richer and for poorer . . ." That is faithfulness.

Sometimes we may chafe at our commitments, and feel that we are no longer free, but true freedom requires respecting boundaries and commitment. If people cannot rely on you, you will not be trusted or respected, and that will curtail your freedom. If you make commitments to yourself and don't keep them, your sense of integrity and self-esteem will be impaired, and you will have lost something profound: the freedom to be whole.

You must also be faithful on the *dojo* floor. Perhaps you relax when your instructor isn't looking. You are cheating yourself of course; but have you considered what it does to the morale of your fellow students? The instructor may not notice you, but the other students might, and you will lose their respect, and may even demoralize and influence them to cheat as well. Always give your best effort, even when you think no one is looking.

Being faithful means aligning our thoughts and words with our deeds. We say the *Dojo Kun* after every class. Are you being sincere when you say the words "be faithful"? Were you honorable on the *dojo* floor today? If you weren't, then when you are saying the *Dojo Kun*, you are being doubly insincere. You now know that karate is for the perfection of character. Are you committed, and are you faithful?

Endeavor
Doryoku no seishin o yashinau koto

You must cultivate the spirit of endurance. You can not see this kind of spirit with your eyes, but the serious karate practitioner will have reserves of spirit in his or her later years that are manifest to all. Medical scientists tend to say that strength and skill decline after age 25, but I say that with martial arts, one can continue to grow. If you endeavor, you will endure.

I came to America in my thirties, and I was at my best physically. Yet by 40 years old, I had acquired the greatest feeling of confidence and competence. Every year, as I get older, I continue to challenge myself. Every six months, I go for a physical, and the doctor tells me that I'm different than most men even 30 years younger: healthier, slimmer, stronger, faster, more limber, and happier too. I say this not to boast, but to tell you that it is because I am a martial artist. In most sports, the coaches are too out of shape to play the game. Once I cannot demonstrate techniques myself though, I will have to retire. Master Funakoshi taught until he was in his eighties. I am now 75, and I practice every day for at least one hour, with the exception of a day or two a week to rest. I tell my students to practice for at least 10 to 20 minutes every day by at least doing a sequence of basic moves that incorporate all Shotokan karate stances. Within a few minutes of starting, your mind will become clearer, which will enable you to function more effectively throughout the day.

To endeavor means to always work towards your goals. It means making sacrifices for them, and it may even mean forgoing conventional rewards and acclaim. Ideally, we endeavor because we are committed to perfecting our character above everything else. Every aspect of life, however, requires this level of dedication and seriousness. If we're not working on moving forward, we're falling behind. There is no such thing as even treading water without making an effort.

Even a master must never cease to endeavor, for even a master is not perfect. When people call me master, I'm uncomfortable, because I'm certain that I'm not good enough yet: I can always improve. There are three categories of teacher in Shotokan karate: *Kyoshi* means teacher or instructor; *hanshi* is above *kyoshi* and means expert teacher; and *shihan* means master teacher. If I was like Master Funakoshi, then yes, then I could be a master– but no way! I can barely touch his toes! So, I still endeavor to be like he was.

Respect others
Reigi o omonzuru koto

A true martial artist always shows respect to other people. This is something that you ought to feel in your heart. Showing respect is a sign of humility, and humility is necessary for an open mind, which in turn is necessary for you to learn and grow. You can always learn something from everyone that you meet. Everyone you encounter is a potential friend or opponent, and could either pose a benefit or danger to you. If you respect everyone though, you will be able to see things for what they are, and you will be able to get the most from every experience.

You must always show respect to everyone regardless of ranking, and even when it is difficult. Respect is shown through bowing and through courtesies. *Reigi* means both respect and etiquette. Respect must be demonstrated; otherwise it is as if it doesn't exist.

For example, sometimes in a class, a student may make a mistake. If I yell at him or her, the student may get upset. However, if I say, "No one's perfect. Try not to make that mistake again," then the student will be able to accept my criticism, because I have shown him or her respect. But if someone intentionally hit someone else or is continually not paying attention, I wouldn't say it that gently. Respect also demands truth telling and reprimanding.

After I graduated from Takushoku University at age 21,

I received my *sandan* (third level black belt) from Master Funakoshi. At that time, all the martial arts masters in Japan would get together for public demonstrations. They understood and respected each other, because they were all equals, both mentally and physically. They often discussed how to develop a real understanding of the martial arts in their students. They all wanted to learn from each other. They all took the attitude of, "I'm not good enough; I can always learn something new." After these demonstrations, I would drive Master Funakoshi home, and he always praised the other masters, "They are the best," he would say.

You may think it curious that "respect others" is the fourth principle. Why is it not the first? Isn't this the most important ethical principle? Yes, it is very important, however, before you can respect others, you must respect yourself. True self-respect only comes after understanding that both karate and life are for the perfection of character, and after committing to faithfully endeavoring to keep one's commitments along this road. Only this kind of person can truly respect others, and command the respect of others.

If you have not acquired self-respect, you will not even be able to recognize the qualities that deserve respect. If you have never attempted to improve your character or haven't even realized that doing so is the goal, you will be self-satisfied, and thus you will not be humble. Once you start aiming to become better, and you realize how difficult it is, and how far the distance is between who you are now and where you ought to be, then you will become humble. Only someone who is humble, and knows that he or she is imperfect, is truly on the road to perfection, and is truly worthy of respect and capable of respecting others.

When you are humble and respect others, you will always admit fault, always give the benefit of the doubt and judge others favorably, and will always apologize when you have erred. If you do not feel respect, then you must cultivate it. Start first by taking the *Dojo Kun* seriously, and trying to become a respectable person yourself. Do not wait, however, to become a better person before you start being courteous and showing respect to all. Even if you don't feel this way inside, force yourself to be that way on the outside, and gradually, through externally being gracious and respectful, you will become so on the inside. Perhaps you feel this is insincere? It is not insincere. It is respectful, and it can never be insincere to behave the way that your highest self would behave. As you become externally and internally more respectful, you will also become more worthy of respect.

Refrain from violent behavior
Kekki no yu o imashimuru koto

This is a reminder to remain calm inside. Inner conflict is a form of violence. It can lead to violent action, which is something you should try to avoid at all costs. A martial artist must always be in control, and control begins with an inner calmness, with peace of mind.

This principle is actually telling us to avoid foolhardy courageousness and getting caught-up in the fury of the moment. It is telling us that we must remain balanced, poised, and calm at all times, and never act rashly.

Master Funakoshi always strove to refrain from violence. Once I was with him on a train in Japan, and a man pick-pocketed him. Master Funakoshi caught his arm, twisted it, and said quietly "Don't do that again." That was it. He never turned him over to the police. He did not let anger take control.

It may seem to you as if "refrain from violent behavior," like "respect others," ought to come higher in the list of *Dojo Kun* principles. Let me ask you though: If you have no interest in perfecting yourself, if you are not humble, if you are not faithful, if you do not endeavor, and if you do not respect others, then what sense will it make for you to refrain from violent behavior? Of what use will it be to speak of self-restraint and discipline? Yes, everyone, even people who lack these characteristics, must not be violent and must be prevented from and punished for being violent. We, on the other hand are martial artists. We strive not to let our physical and emotional desires and impulses dictate the way we act. This is why Master Funakoshi gave us this as the fifth of the master principles in the *Dojo Kun*. It is a principle for a peaceful warrior.

Niju Kun

The *Niju Kun* are the twenty subordinate principles of karate. Each one amplifies an aspect of one or more of the broader *Dojo Kun* principles. It takes time to integrate a principle fully into one's mind and life. Therefore, I suggest the following methodology for learning and assimilating these precepts:

1. Set aside 10 minutes a day and establish a regular time and place for studying these precepts.
2. Clear your mind before reciting them.
3. Recite each precept out loud and with emotional power and conviction. Saying something out loud makes what you read more vivid and easier to remember.
4. Recite the 20 precepts in order.
5. Then, read aloud the chapter on the first precept. Concentrate on what you are reading. Each study session, for a week, recite the same chapter, reading it each time as if it were the first time. Repetition is essential, just as it is with a *kata*, in order to make the precept part of your mind so that it becomes automatic.
6. During the course of each day, look for ways to apply the precept.
7. The next week, each day, after reciting all precepts of the *Niju Kun,* repeat briefly to yourself what precept one

means, and then read the chapter on precept two.

8. Each week, begin a new precept and repeat the process.

9. After twenty weeks and twenty precepts, start over!

1

Do not forget that karate begins with a bow and finishes with a bow

Karate-do wa rei ni hajimari rei ni owaru koto o wasureruna

Just as karate begins with a bow, so too does Master Funakoshi's *Niju Kun* begin by telling us this very principle. *Rei*, literally translated, means salute, salutation, or bow. The way that you begin something can set the tone for the entirety of the endeavor, encounter, or relationship.

From the very first karate class, the *karate-ka* (one who practices karate) learns how to bow properly. This simple physical action of bowing embodies the wisdom and goal of karate, and non-verbally re-summarizes the five principles of the *Dojo Kun*. How? Bowing implies humility. Humility indicates a person who is working hard towards the perfection of character. Bowing indicates honoring the spirit of karate, which suggests faithfulness to an ideal. Bowing demonstrates a willingness to learn and to endeavor, to literally make the body subject to its will. Bowing conveys respect for the art of karate, respect for a master or *sensei*, respect for the self, and respect for an opponent. Bowing implies a commitment to refrain from violence.

When you bow to an opponent, prior to any type of *kumite* (sparring) endeavor, you should be saying to yourself, "I am not attempting to destroy my opponent; I am not fighting from animalistic instincts; I am able to pause before I strike; I am engaged in this situation only to practice defending myself, nothing more. And by showing you the top of my head, I am showing that I trust and respect you, and that I am willing to step back and bow again after the encounter concludes."

Learning the correct form for bowing is essential so that we may express proper feeling. There are two types of bowing in karate. The first is from a standing position. This is called *ritsu-rei*. The second type is from the *seiza* (kneeling, or correct sitting) position. This is called *seiza-rei*. In both forms of bowing, you must always strive to feel and exude respect and humility towards everyone, from the greatest master to the freshest beginner.

When bowing, do so from the waist, lowering the head. Do not look up at your opponent; to convey respect, you must convey trust. At the beginning and ending of a karate class, while we are in *seiza,* we close our eyes to meditate after the command *mokuso* (meditation) is given, in order to open our minds for greater awareness and intuition. This, like everything else valuable in karate and in life, takes time to develop. It is a kind of "sixth sense" that is being developed by momentarily taking our eyes off of our opponent, which permits us to be courageous, humble, and respectful.

When I am in *seiza* during *mokuso*, my eyes are slightly open. I gaze about three feet in front of me. I repeat to myself, "*mu, mu, mu*," which is the shorter version of *mushin* (empty mind, or no mind). With the head down, humility is experienced, and when one is humble, more can be perceived and learned. Students who truly focus on this principle are different. I can feel it when they bow to me. When a student bows to their instructors or their *senpai* (their seniors), it is a way of saying from the heart and soul, "I need more help; I need more practice."

Many *karate-ka* have forgotten about *rei*, and do not bow with this spirit of humility and respect; they are focused almost solely upon winning tournaments. I have said this many times before: "If you do not show courtesy, you are not a true martial artist." Yes, karate is technically a fighting art, however, we must distinguish the human being (who has reasoning power), from the animal (who acts solely on instinct). The true *karate-ka* understands that fighting is a last resort, and that having to fight at all, with the exception of an unprovoked self-defense situation, is to fail as a human being. It is the cultivation of respect and humility that makes us human, not the cultivation of aggression.

You can learn something from everyone and from every experience. So, always treat everyone and everything as you would your *sensei*: with respect. Even your enemies are worthy of respect, for they could be great teachers.

Sometimes people don't want to bow for religious reasons. Bowing is not a religious expression for a martial artist. In showing respect through *rei* to your *sensei*, your *senpai*, your *kohai* (junior), your opponent, or someone you encounter in everyday life, you are showing that person your willingness and desire to learn from them, and that person will most likely respond with respect. That person can help you. People who have many good friends usually understand and practice the principles of *rei*.

When we bow before and after a *kumite* match, we are declaring that we respect the power and skill of our opponent. Without this respect, we will not be engaged at 100 percent of our capacity, and thus may become careless and be defeated. Having humility does not mean that we are to think that we cannot win, and that our opponent is better than we are; it means that we must shed all preconceived notions about our opponent and ourselves, and that we nullify our egos so that our minds become focused on not being defeated, rather than on showing off and being over-confident, which are great hazards.

In Western society, people customarily shake hands rather than bow. Shaking hands originated as a way of saying "I come empty handed, I have no weapon," and has come to be merely a way of saying hello. Yet, like bowing, it can communicate a lot about a person. It can convey warmth, strength, conviction, friendliness, and their opposites; however, respect and humility are much harder to convey through a handshake than they are through a bow. Perhaps this is because a bow does not require physical contact and, therefore, is a truer expression of feeling. A handshake though, may become an opportunity to assert one's personality or even to intimidate; with a bow this is a virtual impossibility. Still, shaking hands is a form of politeness and good manners in Western cultures, just as bowing is in Eastern cultures.

Politeness and respect also take the form of verbal expressions such as "please," and "thank you," and "excuse me." These expressions can be considered a form of *rei*. We live in an increasingly informal society where people often neglect the niceties of respect or perform them without conscious intention. Karate and *rei* bring these things back to the forefront of consciousness. When we bow, we need to consciously focus on the form and meaning of the bow and *rei*, so that we can communicate effectively, and even more importantly, shape ourselves to conform to the spirit of bowing and *rei*. The true martial artist attempts to bring this awareness and conscientiousness to every aspect of life.

What we do externally, whether consciously or unconsciously, forms and modifies our psyches. The person who bows carelessly, who acts and speaks carelessly, or who does not address others with respect and humility, increasingly becomes a person who is internally (actually) oblivious, arrogant, and disrespectful. On the other hand, the person who consciously bows, addresses, and treats people with respect and humility (even if that person initially doesn't necessarily feel that respect and humility) will increasingly become a person who is truly respectful and humble.

So, by beginning the *Niju Kun* with this principle, Master Funakoshi has taught us this very profound lesson: that what we do is who we are. There is no room in karate, or in life, for the separation of deeds and character. The goal of being a *karate-ka* is to completely unify your mind, body, and deeds for the good, and thus bring harmony into the world.

2

In karate, never attack first

Karate ni sente nashi

Karate is a physical art. We block, punch, kick, and strike in order to practice defending ourselves. Yet one of the main goals of practicing karate is to remake ourselves into non-violent beings. It isn't accidental that, while training, the first move that we make from *shizen tai* (ready/natural position) is a block, and that each *kata* begins with a blocking technique. Even though blocks can be considered strikes and strikes can be considered blocks, we must understand that an effective block directed at a vital point on the arm or leg of an attacker can instantly end the encounter. This emphasis on blocking and on not attacking first reinforces the philosophy of non-violence.

The principle is integrated into the deep structure of our martial art. Experienced *karate-ka* know that by discovering an opponent's strategy, they can anticipate and follow his or her movements, and more easily defeat him or her. To do this, you must put ego aside and clear your mind. This way, if there is an opening for an attack (be aware that in tournament or *dojo kumite*, you must always consider yourself already under attack), you will see it, utilize it, and be able to stop your opponent.

Also, never attacking first does not mean that you cannot strike first if you absolutely know you're going to be attacked. Practicing this principle of "never attack first" enables us to immediately see and seize opportunities. An "attacking mind-set," in contrast, is one in which the ego can blind us to seeing opportunities and dangers.

In life, as in karate, we must recognize and seize opportunity before the chance is gone. *Karate ni sente nashi* is about cultivating one's ability to react to a situation. You must fully "see" your situation and be able to react appropriately and instantaneously. If you do not train diligently, you will never grasp the essence of this principle.

The question arises: is this principle meant simply to help us win competitions, or is it an ethical principle, meant to help us become better people and, consequently, make the world a better place? Like the most profound of principles, it is both. If some precepts were to help one win, but required unethical behavior, they wouldn't be true principles. If the practice of some precept caused one to be defeated and not learn from the situation, it too would fail to be a true principle. This is not to say that adherence to a true principle will never be difficult nor cost a person anything. The true test of one's character comes under pressure and amidst conflicts of interest. Many people abandon principle when the "going gets tough." Ethical principles should always transcend and cancel-out practical principles, but some principles, like *karate ni sente nashi*, are very powerful because they are both ethical and practical.

A true martial artist avoids conflicts as much as possible; however, if conflicts do arise, he or she should face them with dignity, and as peacefully as possible. More than merely refraining from violence, the *karate-ka* prefers the way of peace, strives to be friendly and respectful to everyone, and looks for opportunities to help and serve others.

It might seem that in the real world this principle of never attacking first is impractical. In business and politics, for example, it may seem necessary to always be on the offensive; always be the first to attack; always be the first to market. This is an inaccurate understanding of life though. Voters and consumers appreciate quality, dignity, and respect. The political candidate who avoids mudslinging and who simply sidesteps or deflects the insults and accusations that are thrown his or her way is far more impressive than his or her opponent. The cutthroat businessperson who cuts corners on quality to be the first to the marketplace, and who defines himself or herself in contrast with his or her competitors lacks both self-respect and respect for others. It is the businessperson who carefully observes and analyzes the marketplace, takes the time to develop and produce a quality product or service, respects partners and competitors, treats employees respectfully, and respects customers who will ultimately succeed in the long run. Never attacking first does not mean being passive or being a victim; it means being wise and strong. It means making sure that right is on your side.

A great secret of karate is that through diligent training, you become so confident and competent that you can afford to be magnanimous and cede the way to others without making a big deal about it. You need neither tremble before, nor tyrannize over anyone, for you have become wise and strong. Only the weak cower, and only the weak are bullies. Humility is different than weakness; it is rooted in confidence, skill, and strength.

3

One who practices karate must follow the way of justice

Karate wa gi no tasuke

Justice means doing right and allying with the right. A *karate-ka* must help and defend all who require such assistance. In less grandiose terms, justice is about doing things in the right way. In karate, both senses of the meaning are significant.

As a *karate-ka*, your responsibility to others increases. You are no longer permitted to remain an innocent bystander to an act of physical aggression against another person without intervening to defend him or her. Conversely, because you have such knowledge and power, and could easily hurt someone with it, you are obligated never to use more force than is necessary to stop aggression. Justice is a tightrope. It takes someone of great skill, humility, self-awareness, sensitivity, and moral restraint to walk it.

In karate, when you practice things such as *kihon* (basics), *kata*, or *kumite*, you must learn to do them the proper way from the beginning. You must be straight and honorable with yourself and with your *sensei*; you must be practicing justice. Don't relax when your *sensei* is not looking your way. Don't hold back on your efforts. No one else may know that you have slacked or shirked but you; justice demands truth, and the person who is not honest with himself or herself is not going to be honest to others.

When you practice, you may make mistakes and you

must hope that others will give you the benefit of the doubt and be just towards you. So too, when you are sparring, someone may hit you accidentally. Of course excessive contact is wrong, but if you retaliate, this is not just. Justice requires tolerance and forbearance. Find a way to ensure your opponent does not do it again, and convey your understanding that a mistake was made. You will both benefit that way.

Understanding and practicing justice should be inseparable. Unfortunately, all too often, knowing the path is one thing, and walking it is another thing altogether. Fulfilling the principle of justice requires physical and mental strength, hard training, and pride tempered by humility. Our thoughts and feelings are powerful and can lead us to do things which we know to be wrong. The pull of society is also very strong, and when all of society is doing that which is unjust, it is very difficult for a person to stand against the tide of opinion and risk ridicule or oppression in order to live the ideals of justice. As *karate-ka*, we must resist and stand against the tide.

Karate trains us to develop a strong, independent spirit. It enables us to develop the inner strength to attach ourselves to enduring and true principles of justice. Karate integrates body, mind, and soul. It breaks down the ego, which speaks only to self-interest, and brings forth our true moral essence of spirit. Karate allows us to embody and employ justice in this world.

4

Know yourself first, then you can know others

Mazu jiko o shire, shikoshite ta o shire

This principle has two components, and achieving the latter is impossible without achieving the former. First let's examine the principle in the broader context of application in daily life.

The quest to know one's self entails intense introspection, through which we first seek to draw out our motivations and intentions, our influences and the events that have shaped us, our beliefs and principles, our goals, our purpose in life, our talents and skills, and our weaknesses and flaws. Identification of these things is only the first step to the first component of this principle.

The second step involves evaluating the quality of these things: are our motivations and intentions proper ones? Were our influences negative or positive, and are we bound to be limited by them? Are our beliefs and principles true, and are we living our lives in accord with them? Have we capitalized upon our talents to the best of our capacity, and used them to make the world a better place?

The third step to the first component of "know yourself, then you can know others," is that we must realize that we can implement change: we can purify our motivations and intentions, rectify our faulty beliefs and principles, and bring our thoughts and actions into accord with what we believe. We can work diligently to improve upon our strengths and develop our skills, and to eliminate or work around our weaknesses. It is only once we've become steadily and thoroughly engaged in this process that we can really come to understand others. One of the paradoxes of being human is that we are all unique and yet we are also all the same. Thus, once you understand the number of ways that your own body and mind can sometimes fail or deceive you, you will understand how others think as well.

I have been speaking of knowing yourself in a universal sense, yet knowing yourself solely in relation to karate is something slightly simpler. In karate, we work hard to eliminate the great impediment to self-knowledge: the ego. This is why we emphasize the development of humility through karate training. When you bow; when you do *soji* (cleaning); when you respectfully say *osu* to your fellow students and instructors; when you say "thank you," to your opponent after *kumite*; when you accept the fact that you can learn something new in every class you participate in; when you realize that a perfect technique is impossible; and most importantly, when you realize that you are not separate from anyone else, you are developing humility. You are breaking down your ego, and developing your ability to see yourself clearly, recognize your weaknesses, and identify and develop your strengths and spirit.

To get ego out of the way, you must practice suppressing it at all times. A great way to do this, as I mentioned, is to always remember that we are not separate from one another. Your fellow students and instructors, although each at different levels in their development, are training in karate for many of the same reasons you are training. Additionally, when you bow humbly, shy away from honors, assume greater responsibilities, and know that you could have done better, you are not only eliminating ego, you are aligning yourself with all who you encounter, which will ultimately make the world a better place.

It is critical that karate instructors understand this fourth principle, and demonstrate a good example to their students and to others and assume greater responsibility. If my students are not learning, for example, I always know that it is my fault. Once you are high ranking, you must practice even longer and harder. I train hard five to six days a week, every week. When people begin to think that they are good, their mental and physical discipline begins to decline. You must keep training because once you stop, your skills will atrophy. Never become self-content! That is just ego and false confidence. As we get older and develop more skill, we may arrogantly think "I have more experience; those young students don't know anything." This arrogance is dangerous.

Always proceed on the assumption that you are not perfect, that you have not learned enough, and that everyone has something that they can teach you.

Knowing yourself means knowing the difference between the person you ought to be, and the person that you are right now. Master Funakoshi was the most humble human being I have ever known. He was a true martial arts master. He was also a brilliant writer, poet, and philosopher; and someone who brought the world *Shotokan* karate, and the *Dojo Kun* and *Niju Kun*. And yet, up until the day he passed away, he always believed that he had much more to learn. I strive to emulate his humble characteristics. Every day I train, I start back at the beginning, as a white belt. I too, still have much to learn at 75 years of age.

After a tournament, some *karate-ka* complain about how the judges missed a punch or a kick in a *kumite* match, or that they didn't judge a *kata* fairly. Complaining is a waste of time. Instead, return to the *dojo* with an iron resolve to train harder and work on those areas that don't come easily, and make sure that the techniques are so accurate that no judge could possibly miss the point. True champions never complain. They are humble. They can see their weaknesses, and they resolve to mend them.

When you know yourself, then you will understand your

level of training and technical ability. You will understand your physical limitations and how to work around them and improve them. You will see the mental traps which you fall into, such as laziness and dishonesty; and you will have learned how to avoid them. You will also be able to anticipate the way that a competitor or a real-life attacker will attack, and you'll be able to gauge their intentions. You will be a complete martial artist.

Teaching is a wonderful tool for learning more about one's self. Through the act of demonstrating and explaining how to do something properly, one discovers new aspects to what is being taught that he or she did not understand previously. The teacher benefits as much from the interaction as the student, becoming both wiser and humbler.

Do not hoard your knowledge: if one of your fellow students is weak, help him or her. Do not fear that if you help, the student will surpass you, or beat you in the next tournament. Remember, you are only truly competing against yourself, to make yourself better, and helping someone else makes the both of you better. It is that simple. Whether you win or lose in a tournament is ultimately irrelevant. On the other hand, if you have a weakness in your training, you must seek instruction from those who are better than you. No one can be the best in everything. We must all help each other, and make one strong unit.

The key to success is not worrying about other people's opinions, or their progress, or the things that they do which upset you; these are distractions. As long as you focus on comparing yourself to other people, you will never come to know yourself. Karate is not about being better than anyone else, but about striving to being better than you used to be both as a person and as a martial artist. Know yourself. Know others. Help others. This is the way of *karate-do*.

5

Spirit and mind are more important than technique

Gijutsu yori shinjutsu

The toughest physical labor is easier than spiritual mastery. Master Funakoshi understood that it is human nature to prefer strengthening physical skills to developing spirit and mind, and yet he believed that this misplaced focus is tragic, for spiritual development is the essence of karate, and technical skills are merely the means to this end. Master Funakoshi isn't saying that physical skills are unimportant, but spirit and mind are what set us apart from the beasts.

In a *kata* competition between two people with comparable skill levels, it is the person with more fire in his or her heart, emanating more *ki* (energy), and with the cooler head, who will most likely be victorious. Often, a fighter with great spirit and mind can even defeat an opponent with better technique and more experience.

Spirit is often communicated through *ki-ai* and *kime*. *Ki-ai* is the powerful shout from a *karate-ka* at certain critical points when he or she makes focus (*kime*) while executing a technique. *Ki-ai* is the point at which one's *ki* unifies and gels body and soul. The word *kime*, is a contraction of the word *kimeru*, which means decisiveness. Naturally, the *karate-ka* with both maximum skill and spirit is always the superior one; and while it is possible that one might be very skilled but lack spirit and mind, it is unlikely, for these things tend to develop together.

Japanese marital arts use the suffix *"do"* (*Karate-do, Kendo, Judo, Aikido*), which means "the way" and emphasizes that spiritual growth and perfection of character are the objectives of the practice of martial arts. The word *michi*, which is used in the second precept of the *Dojo Kun*, may be used interchangeably with *do*, as it has the same character: *do* is the Chinese reading, *michi* is the Japanese reading. A person of any age or size can learn karate, because as a martial art, karate implies the development of *shinjitsu* (spiritual skill and development), which continue over a lifetime, as opposed to physical development, which will always have limits for everyone.

Spirit is the essence of our being, our personality, and our motive force. Mind is that which harnesses and channels our spirit towards growth and towards physical manifestation of our desires and goals. Mind is also that which thinks and controls the body through the brain. The brain is not the thinker, it is what the thinker uses. Neither spirit, mind, nor body act in isolation. Every impulse of our soul, every thought we think, and every act we do are all intricately linked and alter us permanently at every level. Karate is a holistic martial art, which aims at reforming and perfecting the entire person.

Karate can give you neither spirit nor intelligence.

Karate simply provides a structure in which you can develop your inherent spirit and mind through the practice of acquiring and refining physical techniques for self-defense. One first has to have the desire to learn karate and decide to go to a class; this alone takes more spirit and mind than most people have.

Spirit and mind continue to be made manifest in the students who doggedly persist: who show-up to class regularly and practice every day. It is shown in the way students hold themselves; in the sincerity with which they bow; in the way that they treat other people; in the way in which they shun boastfulness; in the way they sustain enthusiasm day in and day out, always keeping a positive attitude towards working, and towards accepting instruction; and in the way that they pay close attention to the details of form and technique. While training, even when you are exhausted and feel unable to do any more, you must persist and let your spirit take over. Determination and discipline can conquer the greatest opposition. In life too, the greatest rewards are attained by those who persist despite all obstacles. Never give up!

When I was young, and started learning the martial arts, my initial motivations were no different than those of most beginning practitioners. I wanted to learn how to be the best fighter: to be strong, fast, and lethal. Slowly and subtly, karate changed me, and I came to value the more spiritual aspects of the practice. I am 75 years of age now, and I still work hard every day. I know that I am not yet good enough, and that I must always strive to be better.

If you are aware of the importance of the mental and spiritual aspects of karate from the beginning though, the transformation won't surprise you, and your knowledge of the true goal will accelerate your spiritual development.

6

Be ready to release your mind

Kokoro wa hanatan koto o yosu

As I mentioned in the first principle of the *Niju Kun*, *mushin* means empty mind, or no mind. Only if you can release your mind, will you be able to release your body for the right movement at the right moment to defend yourself against an opponent.

Although you must always concentrate fully upon what you are doing in the present moment, you must also be ready to react to any sudden change in your situation. The one constant in our lives, externally, is change. Conversely, the one constant in our lives internally, must be adherence to our principles and core beliefs, so long as they have been chosen honestly, tested, and have been proven to be true. The *Dojo Kun* and *Niju Kun* have stood the test of time, and have been shown to be accurate and reliable, and this is why we repeat the *Dojo Kun* after every karate session: we wish to internalize it in the bedrock of our soul, so that when we release our minds, we are still anchored in principle. By being consistent internally, we can be more responsive to change externally.

Releasing your mind means not staying directly attached to it, so that you are able to step back from it and observe it, just as you could an object. You are not your mind, just as you are not that object. At one time or another, you may have heard someone exclaim, "I can't live with myself anymore!" This person is talking about two different selves: "I" and "Myself." How can this be possible?

The "I" is your true self, the self that is able to step back and objectively observe your thoughts and feelings completely, without judgment. The "I" is pure unobstructed consciousness.

"Myself" is your ego, that part of yourself that considers your thoughts and feelings to be actually you. The ego is that which desires gratification, longs to possess things, and which desires the world to be a certain way. It is the source of all human suffering, both individually and on a grand scale, because it is the ego that tells us not to accept what is. This is why the old proverb that "each of us is our own worst enemy" is true: we are divided within ourselves, and our clarity of vision is impaired. By refusing to accept what is, we refuse inner peace, wherein true happiness lies.

In karate, we build competence at each level before a student moves forward. First, we begin with the basics, *kihon*: blocking, punching, kicking, and striking. We first teach *kihon* individually, not in sequences. Then we teach in sequences and combinations, such as *age-uke* (rising block) followed by *gyaku-zuki* (reverse punch). This allows our minds to focus solely on the proper execution of the technique or techniques. Once the student has gotten to the point where these techniques come a bit more naturally, and the mind is ready to expand, the student begins to learn *kata*. Here the techniques are done in set, prearranged sequences, facing imaginary opponents, while applying rhythm and timing. Simultaneously, we teach basic *kumite* such as *gohon kumite* (five-step sparring) and *sanbon kumite* (three step sparring). We then teach *ippon kumite* (one attack/step sparring). Then *jiyu ippon kumite* (semi-free sparring). And finally, once ready (and in our organization, this is only after becoming a first *kyu* (level) brown belt), we allow and teach *jiyu kumite* (free-sparring).

Think about *gohon kumite* and *sanbon kumite*. When we begin learning to spar, though we have already begun to learn *kihon* and *kata*, we have never had an actual opponent. We have no idea of how to adjust our techniques for opponents of different size and speed. We haven't learned how to gauge distance, or how to regulate our timing and coordination. In *gohon* and *sanbon kumite*, as well as in *ippon* and *jiyu ippon kumite*, our opponent calls out the intended move, which gives our mind time to anticipate the move, and in a very subtle way, this subconsciously coaches us visually to anticipate this particular move in the future when the opponent will remain silent. Many people think that intuition in karate is natural, but in fact, it is mostly an acquired skill, and this type of specific karate training accelerates its development.

After one achieves proficiency at *gohon*, *sanbon*, and *ippon kumite*, one can advance to *jiyu ippon kumite*, because one has become better at pacing, distance, timing, and adjusting to the size, speed, and skill of different opponents. *Gohon*, *sanbon*, and *ippon kumite* progressively allow less room for error as the student advances through each level. *Jiyu ippon kumite*, however, leaves even less room for error, less chance to recover, and less chance to evaluate your opponent before he or she strikes. It is assumed that by the time you are practicing at this level, you'll have acquired enough experience and burned enough technique into your muscle memory that your mind will be free enough to allow your body to react more instantaneously and make the proper moves. In *jiyu ippon kumite*, we now engage from a natural stance, in a free-moving, dynamic way, rather than starting from a still position. The attacks, however, are still being called-out in advance. Finally, once proficiency is achieved here, the *karate-ka* is allowed to participate in the ultimate form of *kumite*: *jiyu kumite*. It is at this stage of *kumite* where anything can happen: *Jiyu Kumite* most resembles a real-life combat situation.

We progressively train our minds and bodies to require

less conscious thought for immediate proper response, and every time more brain space becomes available, we refill the space with new information and skill. The mind of a *karateka* is like an infinite reservoir with a small leak which feeds into our body's muscle memory. The leak is slow, but the residue works itself into the body, stays there, and transforms it permanently. The fascinating thing is that the mind never stays full, and that for every bit of skill and knowledge acquired, more mind-water seeps into the body, and a still greater amount of space somehow is made available in the mind. The mind of a master, after decades of practicing karate, is thus vastly open, and yet also contains much more wisdom and knowledge than does an ordinary human being; and yet this wisdom is dwarfed by the empty space. This is how a master can ultimately anticipate any move, and can defeat any opponent. You have heard it said, "the more you learn, the more you know that you don't know." This is why a karate master is so humble: because the master's mind never can regain the illusion of being full that less experienced people often possess. Master Funakoshi was a true master in this respect. This is *mushim*. This is how one "releases the mind."

7

Misfortune comes out of idleness

Waza wai wa ketai ni seizu

Misfortune is the constant complaint of the unprepared, the incompetent, and the lazy. Yes, unexpected things can create difficult, dangerous, or painful situations for anyone; invariably though, the lazy person and his cohorts are the ones most affected, and made most ineffectual by the unexpected.

The *karate-ka* does not blame circumstance for his failings; he or she takes responsibility. The *karate-ka* knows that life involves working diligently day in and day out. It means planning one's days, weeks, and months out in advance, and yet being flexible enough to adapt and alter plans according to principle and circumstance. It means in all things, taking the time to build a foundation of basic skills and knowledge, and to be constantly refining and adding to this base. It means always giving maximum effort in everything that you do. An apparently contradictory, and yet subtle and important point to note is that giving maximum effort may involve conserving effort in order to sustain it. For example, the intelligent *karate-ka*, when in competition against someone of equal or greater skill, will not exhaust all energy aiming for a quick takedown, as he or she knows that the fight is likely to last longer; maximum effort also requires maximal strategy.

Now obviously, if you're attacked on the street you can't

say, "Oh, I'm too tired to defend myself." You must exert every ounce of strength you have, because you don't know to what degree your attacker will go to wound or kill you. You need to attack his vulnerable points immediately and end the fight. Perhaps, if you find yourself evenly matched, you might be able to slow the pace, hoarding your physical reserves while remaining absolutely mentally alert.

So this principle is really about responsibility, but it is communicated in the negative, telling us that when we are irresponsible, we actively generate and attract that which is commonly called, "misfortune." Later, in principle 16 of the *Niju Kun*, Master Funakoshi advises us to be aware that we always have millions of possible opponents; this seventh principle of the *Niju Kun* is telling us that we create and make ourselves vulnerable to many of these opponents: primarily through laziness, un-preparedness, lack of discipline, and overconfidence.

Overconfidence is a subtle manifestation of laziness. Often we think that because we have done something many times, or because it feels easy, we don't have to put out full effort. This is a dangerous attitude. When we do things halfheartedly, accidents occur and people get hurt. There is never an excuse to take it easy on the *dojo* floor.

We all appreciate advanced techniques. Jumping in the

air or performing an intricate *kata* can make us feel powerful and accomplished. Practicing only those techniques is laziness though. We must always practice the fundamentals on which the advanced techniques are based; otherwise, our self-control diminishes as does our ability to control the situation, and misfortune will come. Both basic and advanced techniques require full effort.

In life too, we must always give our all to everything we do. We must never neglect the basics nor become content with our level of competence. One all-too-common pitfall in life, which is a form of laziness, is lack of courtesy, which is the most basic of human social requirements. You should always greet and treat everyone, regardless of social stature, with a pleasant smile, with kindness, politeness, and with respect. This requires conscientious effort. If we neglect to do this, we are sabotaging our own character and we are sabotaging the social stability of our environment.

You should not exclude anyone from your practice of courtesy: neither the postal carrier nor the waitperson, clerk nor cashier, beggar nor billionaire; not your children, not your spouse, not your in-laws, not your friends, and not even your enemies. Common courtesies and the simple tasks in life are the groundwork for the greater things that we wish to accomplish. Even when you are unhappy, it is your obligation to make an effort to be cheerful and friendly: do not spread your misery to others. Don't be lazy. Be courteous to everyone.

8

Don't think that what you learn in karate can't be used outside the dojo

Dojo nomino karate to omouna

Although this is the eighth principle of the *Niju Kun*, I often refer to it first, because it is so fundamental to Master Funakoshi's philosophy of karate. Unless you have picked up this book and have begun reading it here, you have noticed that I talk about this basic idea again and again: whatever you learn from karate has applications in every aspect of your life.

When we recite the *Dojo Kun* after class, we should carry forward our intentions to observe it when we step off the floor and leave the *dojo*. Through daily repetition and resolve to actively manifest these principles in the world, we are more likely to be able to do so. The *dojo* is a training ground for the real world.

Sometimes, well-intentioned family or friends may criticize your devotion to karate. They may ask why you, as a grown person or an adolescent, would "squander" hours of your time practicing karate, when real life and its obligations beckon. "Come on," they'll tell you, "grow up! You'll never need to karate-chop someone, or break a board with your bare hands. It's nice that you have a hobby," they'll say, "but shouldn't you be doing something more productive with your time?"

Perhaps at a time when your level of development has stalled, and you cannot seem to break through to the next level, these condescending jabs will seem plausible to you, and you'll begin to wonder, "Why am I wasting my time at this? Perhaps they are right." This principle tells you though that you must always know that what you learn in karate can be used outside the *dojo*. Never quit practicing, even when you feel your growth is stagnant, and when you have many demands on your time from the outside world. Everyone will likely hit plateaus in their training, where for a long time he or she will not appear to improve. I promise though, that if you persist in training and seek advice from your *sensei*, you will eventually break through.

Karate is the key to functioning more effectively outside the *dojo*. Regardless of whether you put in 15 minutes or an hour a day, this is not lost time. You gain time, efficiency, and energy from practicing karate, and you acquire discipline, skill, self-confidence, and spiritual poise that only benefit you in everyday life. If you practice every day, you will be more productive at work and more helpful at home, and an overall better citizen than if you don't practice every day; and vastly more so than if you give up karate all together.

Sometimes it can be hard to recognize, or easy to forget, the virtues and skills you've acquired from karate. Sometimes it can be hard for those close to you to see clearly, or to understand that karate is making you a better person. If they could look objectively though, un-blinded by emotion and their own egos, they would see that it is in their interests for you to practice karate, perhaps even more than you do now. In Japan, if you are a serious karate student, all the best companies will want to hire you. They want *karate-ka* because they know that karate helps build great character. They know that a *karate-ka* is more productive, reliable, competent, and easier to work with than the average worker.

You mustn't apologize for making karate a priority; and you must be able to explain and demonstrate its utility to other people. The best advertisement for karate is the kind of person you'll become through practicing it. You'll never get there though if you don't stick with it; and not knowing all its practical benefits is one of the traps which can pull you off of the path and cause you to quit. Karate is an invaluable tool for use in real life, and you must never doubt or forget this.

9

It will take all of your life to learn karate

Karate no shugyo wa issho

Karate is not a sport. It is a life discipline. In most sports, a 75 year old coach can no longer compete as a player: the sport was not a way of life for him or her, but merely a passionate pastime. In contrast, any teacher of karate, even if he or she is 90 years of age, must be able to demonstrate that which is taught.

This is part of traditional Asian culture that other cultures often have trouble grasping: respect for elders. Modern society is built upon adulation of youth, rapid change, often-shallow knowledge, and instant gratification. Much of Asia has also been swept-up in this mentality over the past century or so and thus there too, respect for elders is fading. Karate embodies the antithesis of this thinking; it exemplifies a philosophy of elegance, patience, diligence, and respect for tradition and elders, and a *karate-ka* will practice it for life.

It is important to know that the ranking system in karate is not intrinsic to the discipline. Originally, there were no belts, no rankings, and no competitions. The ranking system is a Western influence on karate. As a parallel, before the 20th century, before the *Meiji* restoration, in Japanese schools there was no separation of children by age: no first grade, second grade, and so on.

The danger with rankings in karate, just as with the use of

grades in school, is that we can easily end up thinking that achieving the ranking, or getting the "A," or a college degree, means that we no longer have anything left to learn. The pursuit of these artificial goals can distract us from the real goal, which is to perfect our character, and which will take us until our dying day. The belts, rankings, and rewards do motivate people in the short-term, and that is why we use them; however, Master Funakoshi gave us the *Dojo Kun* and *Niju Kun* to remind us always that karate is about perfecting character, and not about competition and rankings.

When one really understands this principle, he or she will have much more patience with the process of learning karate. Many students enter karate with the mentality that within six months or a year or two, they can become experts. They work very hard, and yet when within that time period, they find themselves still struggling, they often become disillusioned and quit. This is quite sad. It is as if you trained for and entered a marathon, thinking wrongly that it was a 500-meter sprint. You ran the race as fast as possible for 500 meters, stopped exhausted, then looked up and realized that everyone else was still running, yet you could run no more. Had you known the specific kind of race in which you were to be running, you would have trained and paced yourself properly.

Many students strive to get a black belt, and upon receiving one, they think that they have accomplished their goal. But they have lost sight of the real goal: to continue to grow. There is a reminder of this idea in the very name of the rank a student gets upon earning a black belt. The first degree or level of a black belt is called *shodan*. *Sho* means beginning. When you get your black belt, you are in a way, just beginning your journey. Similarly, the ceremony for graduating from college is often called a commencement: a beginning.

In karate, development is often slow. Karate is not about instant gratification. Karate is not an Indian summer, or a rose that blooms briefly then withers. Karate is like a rare tree planted outside of its usual environment, which initially can grow only with careful cultivation. In the early years, its roots need to be insulated from cold weather, and its slender trunk needs to be braced by stakes, and it needs to be watered, pruned, and fussed over. After several years, it can stand on its own, and take care of itself, even though it still has much growing to do. Should no lightening nor gale, no blight nor axe strike it, in 25, 50, 100 years, it will be a giant, solid, deeply rooted, shade-giving, fruit-bearing tree.

Karate, like humankind itself, is a foreign element in the material world: it is a transplant from the world of spirit. For spirit to take root and flourish in the material world, it takes great discipline, great courage, and great wisdom practiced and developed over a lifetime. If you will understand this principle, you will have the proper mindset and perspective: you will not be easily discouraged, and you will certainly grow and develop.

10

Put karate into your everyday living; that is how to see its true beauty

Ara yuru mono o karateka seyo;
soko ni myomi ari

On the surface, this principle may sound similar to the eighth principle of the *Niju Kun*: "Don't think that what you learn in karate can't be used outside the *dojo*," however, there is a key distinction. The eighth principle tells us that we must know that karate can be used in everyday life, whereas this principle tells us that we must actually use it in our everyday life to appreciate it. The eighth principle of the *Niju Kun* is telling us that karate is not limited to the *dojo*, whereas this principle is telling us that it is unlimited in its application.

Why, you might ask, are these two principles linked by the ninth principle of the *Niju Kun*, "It will take all of your life to learn karate," instead of following one after the other? The reason is that only once we understand that it will take a lifetime to learn karate, will we practice enough, and become skilled enough, for our characters to become refined enough that we will even become capable of seeing its true beauty. Without the right perspective, we may only see the hard work of karate in its physical manifestations, whereas its true beauty is much deeper. Karate's true beauty lies in its embodiment of *budo*.

Although karate is a martial art, few of us ever meditate on the meaning of *budo*. This word means to stop conflict. The conflict you must stop is not just that which occurs between yourself and others; more fundamentally, you must stop the conflict within yourself. Only then can you be truly effective in stopping conflict in the external world.

Humans have no real natural physical defenses. Instead, we have the intelligence to create defenses: among them, the fighting arts. Throughout history, it has been necessary to employ these defenses; however if we resort only to fighting to resolve conflicts, humanity cannot survive. This is especially true now, because we have the weaponry to eliminate the entire human race. Just as we must create our own physical defenses, we must also create other, non-violent ways of stopping conflict.

The principles behind the physical techniques we learn in the *dojo* also apply to the rest of our lives, but sometimes the connection is not easy to see. As an example, in *kata* and when turning to execute a technique, our instructors repeat endlessly: "Look first." It is crucial to see what is happening before you react. Similarly, in our daily life, we must observe and evaluate before we act or even speak. I refer to the following proverb, "We each have two eyes and two ears, but only one mouth, in order to remind us that we should look and listen twice before we speak even once."

Often, some of the greatest sources of conflict stem from thoughtless communication. Gossip, lies, and curses can truly wound feelings, wreck relationships, and ruin reputations. Wise people will strive to only speak after having carefully evaluated what they wish to say, making sure that it is kind, truthful, beneficial, and necessary.

While training in karate, we do our best to never make excessive contact. Here again, we learn mental and physical control, which can be applied to other situations in life. We defend, but do not counter without assessing the situation. The ideal is to never need to use our physical skills: to be so calm within, that we are never attacked. When we understand this, we begin to see the true beauty of karate as *budo*.

11

Karate is just like hot water; if you do not give it continuous heat, it will become cold

Karate wa yu no gotoshi taezu netsu o ataezareba moto no mizu ni kaeru

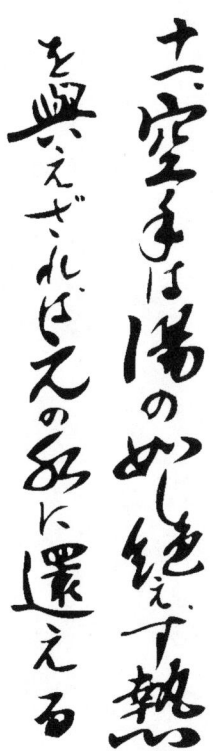

Water dissipates into steam at 100 degrees Celsius. This is its limit. Similarly, the human body has limits. In contrast, the human spirit and mind are virtually unlimited. In one's youth, spirit, mind, and body are energy-dense and developing daily; however bodily ability usually outpaces that of the others. Later in life, the body no longer grows dramatically in ability; however, the mind continues to have the potential to acquire new knowledge. After reaching the maximum level of your ability, you must make an effort to stay there. If you relax with your training, your ability will decrease.

Karate, like hot water, transforms that which it comes in contact with. It is dangerous, and can injure, maim, or kill someone if it is dislodged or expelled from the vessel in which it is kept boiling; though while contained, it is safe. Yet the practice of karate as a way of life transforms a human being into something better than that which he or she was. Water is a medium, a gentle transformer until it is unleashed. Keeping the water of karate hot through practice is the safest way to transform one's self into a better *karate-ka* and a better person. Your imperfections are what are boiled off and converted into energy. Steam, when channeled effectively, can power an enormous locomotive or ocean ship; and the steam of karate, when channeled properly, can power a human life, generating an energy, *ki*, which will permeate every cell of your body, and radiate outwards affecting the world for the better.

The first step of training is to find the time. At minimum, you should train 10 minutes a day, five or six days a week, every week of the year. Not many do this. People aim too high and say, "I will train 30 minutes every day." They then find excuses for missing just one day, and then just two days. If you set the goal at just 10 minutes a day, you have no excuses. How many *gyaku-zuki* (reverse punches) can you do in 10 minutes? With full concentration, speed, and timing? How many *kata*? Just 10 minutes a day of maximum effort will keep you at your level, keep your water boiling. As much as possible, plan to do your 10 minutes of karate in the same place and at the same time every day. Make an appointment with yourself. If you don't, it is easy for you to forget or postpone it.

This principle applies to all aspects of your life. Take at least 10 minutes every day to do something that is important to your life. Maybe it is playing a musical instrument or writing. Whatever it is, do it at least 10 minutes every day. Play your guitar. Swing your golf club. Write a page or two. But do it every day. Schedule it, and do it. So long as you do it every day, you will be able to maintain your level of achievement and keep your water boiling. By thinking of everything as a lifetime endeavor and getting over our desire for instant gratification, we can see that incrementally, bit by bit, day after day, we can build upon the skills and knowledge we've previously acquired.

Water over thousands and millions of years can cut a passage through the hardest stone and can smooth the edges of the most jagged rock. Daily practice similarly cuts a progressively deeper groove into your brain and soul, and finishes off your rough edges. Ten minutes a day might not seem like much, but that's 3,650 minutes of practice a year, or almost 61 hours a year. That's thousands of blocks, punches, kicks, strikes and *kata* each year; and over a lifetime? Over say sixty years? It adds up.

I want to clarify that this 10 minutes of practice a day is of course on top of regular training in a *dojo*, with instruction. Ten minutes is the minimum requirement; but do not attempt more than this until you are consistently doing 10 minutes of practice a day, every day, and then incrementally turn the heat up to 12 or 15 minutes daily. Once you have acclimated to that level of dedication and intensity (and it might take weeks or months to do so,) ratchet-up the heat again. Do not, however, try to start at 15 or 20, or 30 minutes: you'll get scalded! You will get hurt. You will get burnt out. Just make sure that you sustain the heat and never let it cool down; if you do let it cool down, you will find it hard to return to where you were.

For example, if you have been training for five years, and take a year off from training, there is danger in returning. Your reflexes will hunger for applications that your body can no longer withstand. You can easily injure yourself by overextending. Even if you take just a few weeks off, you will be cold when you return; and you must start off slow and at a low heat, and gradually turn the heat back up to where you were before. You will find that karate has not left you; you can even defend yourself in an emergency. When you train regularly, your mind will be ahead of your body. Keep the heat on, always.

12

Do not cling to the idea of winning; it is the idea of not losing that is necessary

*Katsu kangae wa motsuna;
makenu kangae wa hitsuyo*

Master Funakoshi is teaching two very important ideas here. The first is that we must not measure success by something outside of ourselves. We must develop ourselves within, and all of the rest will follow. Understanding this first idea will help you clear your mind, enable you to accept what is, and thereby optimize your ability to react.

Wanting to win is human nature. Yet 'wanting' always puts you off-balance, and causes you to make errors. When you truly understand that you are training solely to better yourself, you will abandon your concerns about winning, losing, advancing in rank, and being attached to results, and you will become a better, more balanced *karate-ka* and human being.

An emphasis on competition will cause you to compare yourself to others, and this is a dangerous way to see things. Thus Master Funakoshi tells us, "It is the idea of not losing that is necessary." Think about it: What will happen if you meditate intently before a match saying to yourself, "I don't have to lose. I am not attached to the result. If I do my best, I will be proud." You will have unburdened yourself of any expectation, and you'll be allowing life to flow naturally. When you empty your mind, you'll be able to discern virtually every intention of an opponent. You won't have an unnatural plan, and your movements will be spontaneous.

Winning means defeating the other person. But "the idea of not losing" means holding on to the objective of making peace: being able to find a solution which does not destroy or humiliate your opponent. "The idea of not losing," means building bridges and making friends, and not putting one's ego ahead of doing the right thing. When one is focused on winning at all costs, all of the principles of the *Dojo Kun* and *Niju Kun* get discarded and trampled upon. The end comes to justify even the meanest of means.

Notice that there is no principle in *Dojo Kun* or *Niju Kun* that says, "winning is everything." In karate, honor and peace are more important than winning. A *karate-ka* has ideally eliminated internal conflict, and thus radiates a contagious peacefulness. If you are a true *karate-ka*, you will be prepared to appear as if at fault, and to apologize rather than create enmity: it is enough that you know that you are likely in the right and yet, because of your humility you can never be completely certain you weren't at least in some way at fault. Avoid conflict whenever possible, and seek for mutually beneficial solutions when conflict can't be avoided.

How are you to integrate this principle into your life, when it is so contrary to the natural human desire to win? You can achieve this only through persistent study of, and meditation upon, these principles and through using them in your devoted practice of karate.

13

Move according to your opponent
Teki ni yotte tenka seyo

With this principle, Master Funakoshi begins to give us general technical principles. He is telling us here to be flexible and adapt to any situation. This takes a lot of experience. When confronted by an opponent, you have to learn how to be physically and mentally connected to him or her. You should be able to perceive your opponent's intentions without distortion. Then you can react naturally, without strategy.

Of course, in dealing with an opponent, you can start out with a strategy, but you should remain flexible so that you can respond effectively. You can't be attached to what you want to do and to what techniques you want to execute. You have to lose your ego and your desire to show off. Just as we learned from the second principle of the *Niju Kun*, "never attack first," one should be primarily reactive until one has adjusted to an opponent, can perceive his or her intentions, and can truly seize the offensive upon sensing an opportunity.

In karate, combat is like a graceful dance, and your opponent is your partner. Just as a dancer must adjust himself or herself to a partner, so too must you adjust yourself to your opponent. You cannot fight someone who is six-foot-four the same way you would fight someone who is five-foot-four. You cannot fight someone who is ultra-fast the way you would an opponent of more average speed.

The idea of moving according to your opponent is yet another of Master Funakoshi's principles that you can apply in everyday life. If you are having a conversation with a friend or a stranger, you need a sense of the other person's intentions, interests, and limits, and need to be able to adapt effortlessly to new scenarios. You need to be able to speak at a level of discourse that the person you are talking with can understand and is comfortable with. You need to adapt to the customs of the locale of which you're in. It takes a lot of experience in working with and talking with other people in order to be effective in this way.

The hidden part of this principle of "moving according to your opponent" is that it takes hard work over many years to get to the point where one can truly put aside ego and move this way. This is why the principle is not introduced right away: integrating the principles that come before it, and building your skill and experience base are prerequisites for being able to implement this one. So keep an open mind, work hard, and don't be attached to your plans and desires: flow with the situation you're in, and move according to your opponent.

14

In conflict, you must discern the vulnerable from the invulnerable points

Tatakai wa kyo-jitsu no soju ikan ni ari

The previous principle was about being able to react and move according to an opponent. This principle is about being able to discern the right moment to switch to an offensive mode of combat. I alluded to this in my commentary on principle 13 by saying that once you have become adapted to an opponent, then you may look for the opportunity to attack; however, just as with the ability to move according to your opponent, attacking effectively requires much experience and training.

Kyo (open) and *Jitsu* (closed) are opposites. In every situation you must be able to distinguish one from the other. For example, *shizen-tai* (natural stance) looks like *Kyo*, when in fact it can be *Jitsu*. Likewise, aggressiveness looks like *Jitsu*, but, it can be *Kyo*. You have to know what you are seeing, and be aware as the situation changes.

When you go in with an attack, always be ready to defend. And when you defend, always have a mind to counter-attack. Master Funakoshi said, "Calm yourself, so you can see in all situations. And when you can see an opportunity, take it immediately."

If you see a target in an opponent, a physically "open" place, you must seize the moment and attack. Remember though, that it is possible that your opponent may only be giving you an illusion of an opening.

So, how do we distinguish between that which is open and that which is closed? We learn from experience, from daily training. In training, we can take chances and not worry about the consequences. Three hundred years ago, I would not have said this, because back then, if you lost, you might have lost your life. Today, we have designed our training methods so that the student can have more opportunities to develop. If you're always worried about going in for an attack, you will never learn what will happen. You will not know what it is to see an opening or to see the danger. Only experience can help the body learn to react and help to discern the vulnerable from the invulnerable. Furthermore, beyond training we need to study. We need to know anatomy so that we know where our opponent's vital points are so that we can defeat him or her more quickly by exploiting weaknesses in combat.

More subtly, with experience you will be able to see the one (*Kyo* or *Jitsu*) inside of and as part of the other. In every seemingly closed situation, there is a vulnerability; and in every seemingly vulnerable moment, there is a capacity for it to close.

In life, we tend to see things as "good" and "bad." We pre-judge life rather than see it for what it is. When we do that, we miss opportunities, and we make ourselves vulnerable. Pre-judging is a function of the ego, not pure consciousness. Pre-judgment is like a cloud, concealing reality, and this is a dangerous liability.

Sometimes, what you think is a "bad thing" is in fact an opportunity to learn, to test yourself, to grow as a person. Say you experience some kind of loss. Because of that loss, you may suffer. As virtually every religion and mythological story reminds us, it is through suffering that a person is often motivated to make positive changes within, to relieve that suffering. When you suffer, you are more likely to take steps away from your egoistic mind. In doing so, you progress towards experiencing *mushin* (empty mind). You learn to accept things as they are, which is what you need to do in order to experience inner peace.

Similarly, something "good" might happen: say you win the lottery. Having won all that money you may, over time, become lazy and self-indulgent; it might increase envy and resentment in your friends and neighbors, and perhaps you will even begin to covet that which previously was out of your reach, and become so materialistic that your inner growth might cease. It has been documented that lottery winners are often unhappier with their lives after winning than they were prior to having won. Wealth, like anything else, must be earned for it to be appreciated.

So it is better for one to clearly perceive that most things are a mixture of "good" and "bad" from the start; and to be fluid enough to react and adapt, and not to get caught up in misapplied preconceptions. Karate trains us to do just this.

15

Consider your opponent's legs and arms as you would lethal swords

Hito no te-ashi o ken to omoe

Here, Master Funakoshi is re-emphasizing the importance of respecting our opponent. Always assume that the opponent poses the ultimate threat to you. Even if you are facing a lower ranking *karate-ka*, don't relax. White belts are sometimes completely innocent; they don't have much strategy or intent, just a technique, and they can hurt even a higher-ranking *karate-ka*. Just a touch of a sword or a knife can hurt or kill you. And if you're facing a higher rank, don't panic. Master Funakoshi always told us, "When the opponent attacks, always think about the weapon. Never think about rank."

Keep your mind the same in all situations: vigilant and open. Any opponent can hurt you, and any opponent can help you to develop and grow as a *karate-ka*. Always, even in practice, treat an opponent's limbs as lethal weapons. To help focus your attention, visualize that your opponent is holding a sharp knife or a sword. This is the epitome of the *karate-ka* mindset.

Of course, once you develop this mindset for your training, don't leave this attitude in the *dojo*. You should always be equally serious in your schoolwork, business, and personal life. Never underestimate anyone; always respect them. When you deal with people, be aware of attitudes, actions, and possibilities. Be ready for anything.

When you are practicing *kata*, concentrate from the beginning. Take the time to create imaginary opponents in your mind. Make them so real that you can actually see their attacks and their responses to your attacks. Create the mindset, "Today they have sharp knives, and they attack with sticks. They strike, grab, and kick. Today someone is coming with a gun." This will impel you to ask the important question, "How do I protect myself?" This will force you to react. Consider too that your own limbs are also like lethal swords. You must never wound someone unnecessarily. You must be humble, avoid conflict, and only attack as the last resort.

This kind of creative visualization process is also invaluable in life. When preparing for any significant venture, if you will have taken the time to visualize successful results achieved through unexpectedly adverse circumstances, this will, in tandem with your acquired skills, make success that much more possible.

Approach everyday life the same way. Words and deeds can wound like swords. Avoid conflicts, but be prepared to deflect an attack if it comes. You make life better both by the small, good actions you do, as well as by those that you don't do because you are aware of your own lethality, whether verbal or physical. Be serious and be careful. Every moment is preparation for the rest of your life.

16

Be aware at all times that you have millions of potential opponents

Danshi mon o izureba hyakuman no teki ari

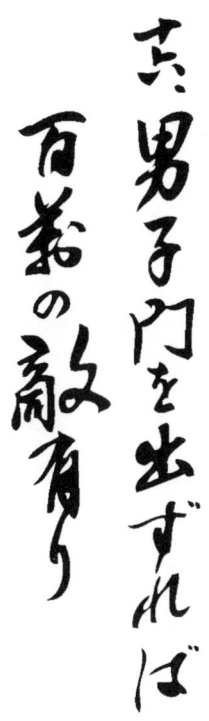

Some students may interpret this principle as advocating extreme paranoia. This is of course not the case. To be paranoid is to project onto reality that which is not real, and we strive for just the opposite. Master Funakoshi is instead teaching us a method by which we can constantly check on our own inner balance. All that he is saying is that you must be vigilant. If you only think about defending yourself while you are training, or are aware of imaginary opponents only when practicing *kata*, then when you leave the *dojo*, you will not be able to effectively defend yourself. You must be a martial artist 24 hours a day.

Master Funakoshi did not mean that when you walk out the door in the morning you must expect that someone will attack you; however, you must be prepared. In karate we say, "Keep your mind like the reflection of water, like a mirror." This means a mind that automatically reflects, sees, and responds to what is around you. When your mind is calm, you're always ready. You develop this capacity through diligent training over a long period of time. Your training, in essence, keeps the mirror clean.

Master Funakoshi said, "Martial arts are about the conflicts within yourself, not with others. Develop yourself so they cannot attack you." If you apply this idea to the principle we are discussing now, he is really saying, "Control yourself at all times." The first thing you have to do to defend yourself is to be in control. So if you imagine that there are a million opponents out there waiting for you, you will have to be present in the moment at all times.

Notice that this principle, like the previous one, is telling us to be ultra-sensitive to possible danger. Principle number 15 of the *Niju Kun* told us that we must treat an opponent's limbs like lethal weapons, and this principle tells us that we must act as if the world is full of opponents. Why has Master Funakoshi made this distinction? He has distinguished between a warning for when we are actively engaged in combat, and one for when we are not actively engaged. When we are engaged in combat, we must be alert and not be careless, and not underestimate the danger. Even more so, when things seem safe, we are likely to relax our guard and become vulnerable. And this is why Master Funakoshi so carefully defined these two principles, which could have less subtly been combined as, "always be aware of potential danger."

Another idea that we should draw out from this principle is that one must always be alert, not just for danger, but for the millions of opportunities that await us to acquire allies and make friends, help others, and to help ourselves as well.

17

Postured stance is for beginners; later comes naturalness

Kamae wa shoshinsha ni atowa shizen-tai

Stance is the foundation of every technique. By executing every technique with a strong stance, you not only strengthen your legs, but you get used to that feeling of stability and optimum power. You have to know how to have the proper weight distribution, foot placement, tension in your body, center of gravity, and the proper posture. Then, as you develop, you can progress to training with a natural stance. In a real-life self-defense situation, that is likely the stance you will have.

What actually happens though, is that after spending many years of training in basic stances, and after you have internalized the basic stance, you are in natural stance all the time. Every move you make will be from a natural stance. There is an old Zen saying: "Before I studied Zen, the mountain was just a mountain; during my study, the mountain was no longer a mountain; and now after studying Zen, the mountain is once more a mountain."

If you are walking in the street when someone attacks you, you are not walking in *zenkutsu-dachi* (front stance); you are walking naturally. As an advanced student, you will be able to execute a strong technique because you have developed your fundamentals; it comes naturally for you. At a certain point in your training, you should have developed something else too: awareness. The advanced student not only has proper technique, but also has hopefully achieved the state of *mushin* (empty mind). Only with a clear mind can a person defend against a sudden attack: even the best techniques will fail without one.

Both training in basic stances and training out of natural stance are important, but the one must precede the other. Develop the foundation first. By training hard and doing the basics from a proper strong stance, you train your mind to focus.

You should always have a clear mind in the *shizen-tai* position. Whether you are doing basics and waiting for the instructor to tell you what to do, or if you are at the beginning of a *kata* or a *kumite* match, let go of whatever is filling your head and relax your body. To someone who doesn't train, it may seem as if you are just standing there, but in actuality you are in a state of heightened awareness. You have the opportunity to do this from the first day of training; even the white belt should be doing this while in *shizen-tai* during basics, or at the beginning of *heian shodan* (the first, or the beginning *kata*/form).

Again, *shizen-tai* means natural position. *Kamae* means ready position. *Shizen-Tai* is a state of "no mind." *Kamae* is a state of being ready to move, anticipating but still without intention. From *shizen-tai*, the body reacts naturally.

Sometimes you don't even know how you move, because the body simply reacts; however, if you don't practice, you will never get to that point. It takes years of training in *kihon*, *kata*, and *kumite* to learn to move naturally from *shizen-tai*; however, it can only be done if you begin with a good foundation.

In life too, we are always anxious to progress, and often will not spend enough time mastering the basics before trying to do the more advanced things. The allure is that it is more fun to just "play" from the beginning. Thus, most people never become experts. They would rather "play" at hobbies, sports, or games than spend the requisite time building a solid foundation. They may have some natural talent, but unless an expert comes along and convinces them to start from scratch, their natural talent will never become a natural-trained talent, which is invariably superior. For natural stance is not really natural- it is trained naturalness: it was not always there, but now it comes naturally.

A beginner's mind-set is so important in karate and in life. We must always try to have fresh awareness, and fresh enthusiasm as if doing it for the first time. We must always strive to recite the *Dojo Kun* with a feeling of deep conviction, and to execute each block, punch, kick, and strike as if it might be the first perfect move we'd ever made, and as if that particular move may save our life. A beginner's mind means living in the present moment.

18

Kata is about correct and proper form; engaging in a real fight is something else

Kata wa tadashiku, jisen wa betsumono

People often misunderstand this translation in that they think Master Funakoshi is saying that *kata* and *kumite* are two different things. In one sense, they are. I always remind my students though, that *kihon*, *kata*, and *kumite* are all part of the same whole.

Kata is the essence of karate. The masters created *kata* by condensing all of karate's techniques to a definite form. By practicing *kata*, you will develop your body movement, rhythm, and timing. You will develop your ability to execute the individual techniques, and you will develop an ability to move naturally from one technique to another. Certain *kata* can be dated back as far as the 15th century, while others are of more recent creation. Strict adherence to proper technique when doing *kata* will lead to natural and effective body movement in combat.

Karate is progressive, and it begins with developing good fundamentals. This is the case with learning *kata*. You have to learn the techniques and movement; simultaneously you must come to understand the meaning of applications within each *kata*, or *bunkai*. In this final step, you need to practice *kata* while keeping imaginary opponents in the forefront of your mind. This will enable you to help prepare mentally for a potential real-life attack situation where you have to respond immediately. Before beginning a *kata*, calm and clear your mind, "find" your opponent(s), then begin the *kata* to practice defending yourself.

In a real conflict, you will never have time to think of which techniques to use; however, if you continually practice *kata*, your techniques will ultimately come more naturally. Your techniques will be strong, rhythmic, connected, and flowing. Ideally, in combat, you will use *kata* techniques unconsciously. It might be slightly different than the exact technique, however, essentially you'll be doing the same thing. Let me give an example: In *heian shodan*, the very first *kata* we learn in karate, every punch is at *chudan* (middle level), to the opponent's solar plexus (imagine that your opponent is approximately the same height as you). The target is a set one, and a punch to any other target while performing this *kata* is a mistake. In a real-life situation though, your open target may be at the *jodan* (upper) level, to the opponent's head. This technique will resemble, but not be the exact technique from *heian shodan*. It will, however, naturally incorporate all you have learned from the repetitive practice of *oi-zuki* (stepping punch) from within this *kata*.

One of the beauties of *kata* is that if you practice *kata* frequently and correctly, you will find different applications for each movement, and these different applications will automatically emerge when and if necessary in a real-life situation.

Once you understand the principles of *kata* movements, you will have a foundation for natural reactions. *Kata* also helps us cultivate spirit. By creating imaginary opponents, you have to muster the spirit for defense; just as in a real life situation, you have to generate spirit on demand. There is a look you'll have in your eyes; a certain force with which you'll make a powerful *ki-ai*, that will let your opponents know that you have a tremendous power within. Practice *kata* throughout your lifetime; and may you never have to use these techniques in a real-life situation.

19

Do not forget:
1) strength and weakness of power;
2) contraction and expansion of body; and 3) rhythm of techniques

*Chikara no kyojaku, tai no shinshuku,
waza no kankyu o wasureruna*

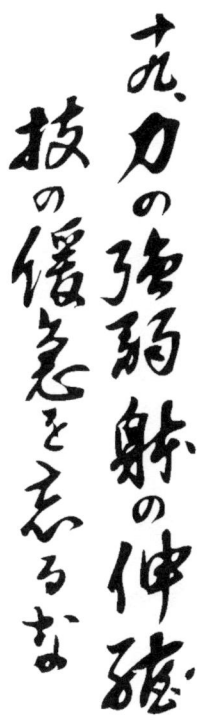

Though these sets of opposites are listed separately within this principle, they are all intricately related, which is why they are bundled together. Try this: sit up straight and pull your arms back as far as you can, trying to touch your hands behind your back. You will notice that your chest expands, while at the same time your upper laterals in your shoulders contract. Everything in the body is linked to both the whole, and to another part of the whole. For every expansion, there is a commensurate contraction, and for every contraction, there is a commensurate expansion.

Expansion and contraction enable you to generate power. When you expand all the way, and then you contract rapidly, there is an explosion of power, like a stone from a slingshot. In *kihon,* we emphasize the expansiveness of each technique in order to develop optimal power. There is a decisive moment after initiating any technique where you contract everything within the body, and *kime* is achieved. After the release of such force and the execution of the technique, the body needs to relax or be "weak" for another split second. You can't have optimal power without contraction, and you can't expand and contract for generating and releasing power without having developed the proper rhythm.

Power takes many forms. It is from relaxation that tension becomes possible and powerful. Life is the same way.

We must learn to understand nature's rhythm and timing in order to see all of power's multiplicity. We need to learn when to give way, and when to push.

The body must breathe in and out; expand and contract. One is not better than the other. Similarly, in life, human beings must be flexible, especially in relationships. Always thinking, "I am right and you are wrong" makes for bad relationships. We need to admit our faults and realize that being right or wrong is not nearly as important as being a good person. Sometimes we should exert ourselves, and sometimes we should retract. If two people are arguing and pushing against each other, change will only be possible if one or both give way a little bit. Maintain that inner sense of balance, so that you'll know the proper action in any situation.

Life has a rhythm. When we are in sync with it, everything flows our way. We develop the ability to be in sync with life by being open, by freeing the mind, and by understanding the pairs of opposites that are balanced within this principle. Some people walk around perpetually tense and stressed and thus they wear themselves out. Yet others are so slack that they barely can muster the energy for daily functioning. A *karate-ka*, however, is the epitome of balance. We've trained ourselves to be responsive to change, we've learned when to tense and when to relax, and how to generate or reduce speed through the proper use of relaxation and tension; and thus we are integrated, optimally-functioning human beings. Life must have balance: hard and soft, positive and negative, fast and slow, yin and yang. Both the body and the mind must work together. This is called *shingi-ittai*. It is the essence of *budo*.

20

Always create and devise

Tsune ni shinen kufu seyo

This last principle is one of the most difficult to translate. What Master Funakoshi is saying is that once the general principle of a technique is understood, then it is up to each person to continually create and devise new applications based on the situation. The best way to look deeper into this is to understand the true role of the *sensei*.

The term *sensei* in Japanese means "one who has gone before" or "one who is experienced." The *sensei* can only explain or demonstrate principles, he or she cannot do the movement for you. Master Funakoshi would demonstrate a technique, or correct us, but he never said, "Copy me exactly." The teacher can only serve as a model for a unique body type. It is your job as a *karate-ka* to find your own way, depending on your own body and mind.

We are still learning so much today about the advanced *kata*. There are no ancient manuals or scrolls detailing movement and application. Therefore, much is open to individual interpretation. Certain applications might work for a taller person, however, they may not work for a shorter person. The important thing is that the principle is always the same. The mechanical action of blocking, punching, kicking, and striking is the same for everyone; however, no one executes a technique exactly like someone else. The instructor can only go so far to explain the feeling of doing a technique properly. Only after many repetitions can a person really start to understand the true and proper movement of a technique. The whole nature of this kind of "understanding" is the essence of karate itself.

Whenever any of us asked Master Funakoshi about a certain technique, he would say, "Do it a thousand times, and then you will get the answer." Of course, few people make the time for that, but I would suggest that you try it yourself. If you want to know how the body should feel when making true *kime*, hit the *makiwara* (practice board) over and over until you feel a strong connection inside. Then you will know that you are beginning to make proper *kime*.

The other meaning of this principle is that you, as a *karate-ka*, must continuously strive to take your karate to the next level. This is the mental aspect to training, and there is no end to this. Only with an open mind can we create something new and be open to learning new things. I am not telling you to create new techniques, what I am saying is that when your mind is open and free of ego, karate then becomes very natural. Use karate to understand yourself, and you will be able to avoid conflict in your life. When there is no conflict in your mind and in your life, then you are really creating and living. This is the true gift that karate can give us all.

Practice hard, and use Master Funakoshi's Dojo Kun and Niju Kun as your guide to both karate training, and life. Keep Training!

Conclusion

Master Funakoshi gave us the *Dojo Kun* and *Niju Kun* to remind us that unless we constantly strive to perfect our characters, we will have missed the point of being martial artists, and will not have lived up to our potential as human beings.

Master Funakoshi created these precepts knowing that science and technology were developing so quickly, that traditional values such as respect and etiquette may be lost in the process. The *Dojo Kun* and *Niju Kun* remind us to incorporate these values into our lives, and to always be aware of our actions and how they affect society and one another.

I will always do my best to strive to pass on the legacy of my teacher, Master Gichin Funakoshi. This is my personal goal and the goal of the International Shotokan Karate Federation. I know if we all do our best to try to live by the *Dojo Kun* and *Niju Kun*, we can all contribute to bring peace to the world.

Glossary of terms found in this book

age-uke . . . . rising block
budo . . . . the way of the martial arts (lit. to stop conflict)
bunkai . . . . application (usually of kata techniques)
chudan . . . . middle level
dan . . . . level
do . . . . the way (Chinese reading)
dojo . . . . training hall
Dojo Kun . . . . The Five General Principles of Shotokan Karate
gohon kumite . . . . . . five-step sparring
gyaku-zuki . . . . reverse punch
hanshi . . . . honorary title for a teacher meaning "expert teacher"
heian shodan . . . . the first kata of the Shotokan syllabus (lit. meaning stable peace, first level)
hitotsu . . . . one characterized by a single horizontal line
ippon . . . . one point
jiyu-ippon kumite . . . semi-free sparring

jiyu kumite	free sparring
kamae	ready position
karate-do	the way of the empty hand
karate-ka	one who practices karate
kata	prearranged forms using karate techniques against multiple, imaginary opponents
ki	energy/life force
ki-ai	a shout from the Karate-ka when making focus (lit. the unification of ki)
kihon	basics
kime	focus (a contraction of the word kimeru)
kimeru	decisiveness
kohai	junior
kyoshi	honorary title meaning "Teacher"
kumite	sparring
kyu	grade
makiwara	practice board for striking (lit. wrapped rice straw)
michi	the way (Japanese reading)
mokuso	meditation
mushin	empty mind or no mind

Niju Kun . . . . The 20 Guiding Principles of Shotokan Karate
oi-zuki . . . . stepping punch
osu . . . . broadly used figure of speech implying respect (in a dojo context)
rei . . . . to bow
reigi . . . . the principles of respect & etiquette
ritsu-rei . . . . standing bow
sanbon kumite . . . . . . three-step sparring
sandan . . . . third level
seiza . . . . to kneel
seiza-rei . . . . bowing from the kneeling position
senpai . . . . senior
sensei . . . . Instructor or teacher (lit. one who has gone before)
shihan . . . . honorary title meaning "Master Teacher"
shingi-ittai . . . . body & mind as one
shin-jitsu . . . . spiritual skill and development
shizen-tai . . . . natural stance
shodan . . . . beginning level or first level
soji . . . . cleaning
zenkutsu-dachi . . . . . . front stance

About the Author

Master Teruyuki Okazaki was born in 1931 in Fukuoka Prefecture Japan, to parents of the Samurai class. Throughout his childhood, he studied *judo* and *kendo*. He began studying *aikido* and karate when he entered Takushoku University at age 16. It was there that he studied karate with Master Gichin Funakoshi, the father of modern karate, and with Master Masatoshi Nakayama, Master Funakoshi's first assistant and co-founder of the Japan Karate Association (Chief Instructor JKA, 1955-1987). Master Okazaki graduated in 1953 with a degree in economics, and subsequently became the coach of the university's karate team. Master Okazaki traveled extensively with Masters Funakoshi and Nakayama, teaching and demonstrating karate to help promote and build the JKA. In addition to his teaching and coaching responsibilities, Master Okazaki helped develop the JKA's first instructor training program.

In 1961, Master Okazaki came to the United States on a six-month teaching assignment in Philadelphia, Pennsylvania. He ultimately made Philadelphia his home and has been teaching and training at the same location for more than 40 years. In 1977, he founded the International

Shotokan Karate Federation and, as its chairman and chief instructor, has built it into a premier karate organization with over 50,000 members in over 30 countries worldwide. He has attained the highest level ranking in Shotokan karate as a 9th *dan* (degree) black belt. He frequently travels throughout the world to teach the technical and philosophical principles of karate to his thousands of students.

For more information about the International Shotokan Karate Federation, please visit www.ISKF.com